Little Mitchie

LET'S LOOK INSIDE A PRAIRIE DOG TOWN

LET'S LOOK INSIDE: ANIMAL HOMES

TRACY VONDER BRINK

CREATING YOUNG NONFICTION READERS

Little Mitchie books spark curiosity and support early nonfiction reading for students in Grades 2-3. Designed to build vocabulary, support second language learners, and prepare readers for middle-grade content, each book includes helpful tips for parents and educators to build confidence and deepen understanding of the world.

TIPS FOR READING NONFICTION WITH BEGINNING READERS

Talk about Nonfiction

Begin by explaining that nonfiction books give us information that is true. The book will be organized around a specific topic or idea, and we may learn new facts through reading.

Look at the Parts

Most nonfiction books have helpful features. Our *Little Mitchie* titles include color photographs and graphic aids, a table of contents, a glossary, and an index. Share the purpose of these features with your reader.

Color Photos and Graphic Aids

A lot of information can be found by "reading" photos, charts, maps, and other graphic aids found within nonfiction texts. Help your reader learn more about the different ways information can be displayed.

Table of Contents

Located at the front of the book, this list shows the big ideas within the text and the page numbers where they can be found.

Glossary

Located at the back of the book, the glossary defines key words and phrases that are related to the topic. These words and phrases can be found in the text in colored type.

Index

Located at the back of the book, an index is an alphabetical list of topics and the page numbers where they can be found.

With a little help and guidance about reading nonfiction, you can feel good about introducing a young reader to the world of *Little Mitchie* nonfiction books.

Little Mitchie is an imprint of:

Mitchell Lane
PUBLISHERS

2001 SW 31st Avenue
Hallandale, FL 33009
mitchelllanepub.com

First Edition, 2027.

Author: Tracy Vonder Brink
Designer: Jen Bowers
Editor: Tricia Hoffman

Library of Congress Cataloging-in-Publication Data
Title: Let's Look Inside a Prairie Dog Town /
by Tracy Vonder Brink

Description: Hallandale, FL :
Mitchell Lane Publishers, [2027]

Identifiers:
ISBN 979-8-89260-874-9 (library bound)
ISBN 979-8-89260-971-5 (eBook)

Library of Congress Control Number: 2026936376

PHOTO CREDITS
Shutterstock: cover, p.1 ©2025 Lost_in_the_Midwest, p.5 ©2011 lightpoet, p.6–7 ©2021 Oleg Kovtun Hydrobio, p.9 ©Jaren Jai Wicklund, p.11 ©2008 David Dohnal, p.13 ©2017 Zoltan Tarlacz, p.14–15 ©2023 Georgi Baird, p.16 ©2010 aabeele, p.19 ©2014 Nick Fox, p.20–21 ©2019 Bella Bender, p.22 ©Fona, ©2025 Vectorial Vision

TABLE OF CONTENTS

Chapter One

PLAYFUL PRAIRIE DOGS

A black-tailed prairie dog stands on a mound of soil. Inside is the entrance to its town. Why is the prairie dog standing there? What's life like inside its town?

Prairie dogs live in **colonies** of hundreds to millions of animals. We call these underground colonies prairie dog towns.

HOME SWEET HOME

The biggest known prairie dog town was 100 feet (30 m) wide and 250 miles (76 m) long. It's thought that 400 million prairie dogs lived there!

Chapter Two

PARTS OF A PRAIRIE DOG TOWN

A prairie dog town usually has 30 to 50 entrance holes per acre. That's about the size of a football field. Prairie dogs dig with their claws. They pile up soil around some of the holes to make mounds. They stand on top to watch for **predators**. The piled-up soil also keeps rainwater from running into the **burrow**. The burrow's main entrance leads to a deep tunnel.

HOME SWEET HOME

Prairie dogs eat the grass that covers the ground above their towns. This not only feeds them but also keeps the grass short so they can see predators and each other.

Shorter side tunnels connect to the main one. They end in **chambers** where prairie dogs sleep, have babies, and hide. Prairie dogs sit in a chamber near the top to listen for predators. Some chambers are used as toilets!

HOME SWEET HOME

Prairie dogs stay cool by going into deep chambers away from summer heat. In winter, the deep chambers keep them out of the cold.

Chapter Three

LIFE INSIDE THE TOWN

A prairie dog group is called a coterie. It's made up of one male, three or four females, and their young. Each coterie has its own **territory** in the town.

HOME SWEET HOME

Females often stay with the coterie where they're born. Young males are chased away to start their own burrows.

Prairie dogs come out when the sun rises. They look for food and eat. Then, they spend the rest of the day **grooming** each other and playing together. They also fix their tunnels and clean their chambers. At sunset, they return to the town to sleep.

HOME SWEET HOME

Female prairie dogs keep their young warm by lining the **nursery** chambers with grass. Baby prairie dogs are called pups.

Some prairie dogs stand guard while the others are outside. If the guards spot a predator, they make a barking sound. When prairie dogs hear the alarm call, they dive into the tunnels and stay there until the danger is gone.

Prairie dogs greet each other by touching their **incisors** together. It looks like a kiss, but it helps them smell each other. That way, they know which prairie dogs are part of their coterie. Or which ones they might need to fight!

The towns aren't just a safe place for prairie dogs. They also help other animals. Rabbits, salamanders, toads, rattlesnakes, and even burrowing owls shelter there. Prairie dog towns can have lots of neighbors!

A LOOK INSIDE

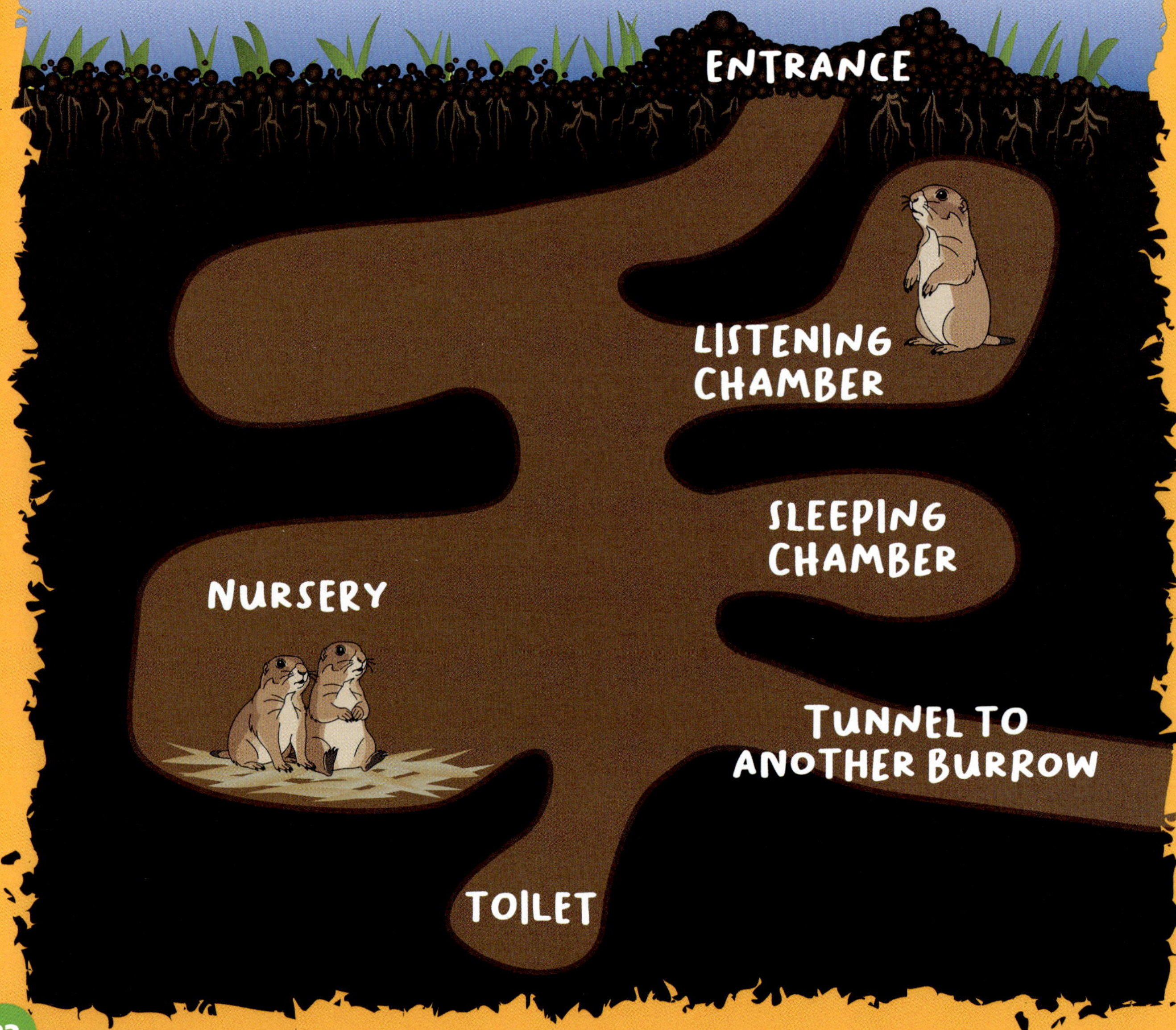

GLOSSARY

burrow (bur-oh) a tunnel or hole in the ground used by an animal

chambers (chaym-burz) rooms

colonies (kah-luh-neez) large groups of animals that live together

grooming (groom-ing) cleaning an animal's fur

incisors (in-sye-zurz) the kind of teeth in the front of the mouth used for cutting

nursery (nur-sur-ee) a place to raise babies

predators (pred-uh-turz) animals that live by hunting other animals for food

territory (ter-i-tor-ee) an area of land under control by a group

FURTHER READING

Duling, Kaitlyn. *Prairie Dogs.* Bellwether Media, 2021.

Patent, Dorothy Hinshaw. *At Home with the Prairie Dog.* Web of Life Children's Books, 2023.

ON THE INTERNET

Prairie Dog

https://kids.britannica.com/students/article/prairie-dog/598805

Find out how big prairie dogs are and watch a short video with Britannica Kids.

Prairie Dog

https://kids.nationalgeographic.com/animals/mammals/facts/prairie-dog

National Geographic Kids shares facts about prairie dogs and how they got their name.

INDEX